A Tribute to the Original,
Traditional,
One-Hundred-Percent,
Red-Blooded,
Two-Fisted,
All-American Christmas...

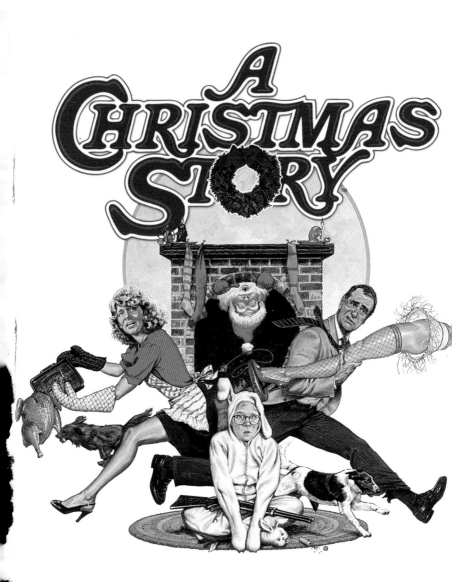

Recipes Courtesy of MyRecipes.com

CAST

Melinda Dillon	Mrs. Parker
Darren McGavin	Mr. Parker
Peter Billingsley	Ralphie Parker
Ian Petrella	Randy Parker
Scott Schwartz	Flick
R.D. Robb	Schwartz
Tedde Moore	Miss Shields
Yano Anaya	Grover Dill
Zack Ward	Scut Farkus
Jeff Gillen	Santa Claus
Colin Fox	Ming the Merciless
Paul Hubbard	Flash Gordon
Leslie Carlson	Tree Man (as Les Carlson)
Jim Hunter	Freight Man
Patty Johnson	Head Elf
Drew Hocevar	Male Elf
David Svoboda	Goggles
Dwayne McLean	Black Bart
Helen E. Kaider	Wicked Witch
John Wong	Chop Suey Palace Owner
Johan Wong	Waiter #1
Fred Lee	Waiter #2
Dan Ma	Waiter #3
Rocco Bellusci	Street Kid
Tommy Wallace	Boy in School
Jean Shepherd	Narrator, Man in Line for Santa
Bob Clark	Swede

Directed by
Bob Clark

Written by
Jean Shepherd

Screenplay by
Jean Shepherd, Leigh Brown, Bob Clark

Release Date: November 18, 1983

 BOB CLARK

Benjamin "Bob" Clark was born in New Orleans and grew up in Fort Lauderdale, Florida. After winning a football scholarship and playing semi-pro for a while, Clark studied theater at the University of Miami – an interest that would fuel his career for the rest of life.

While best known for directing and co-writing the script for *A Christmas Story*, Clark's cinematic roots were planted squarely in independent, low-budget features. His first film, *Children Shouldn't Play with Dead Things* (1972), was a blend of graphic horror and comedy. 1974's cult favorite *Black Christmas* has been cited as a forerunner to the contemporary slasher film by centering its story around a holiday and shooting scenes from the killer's perspective.

But Clark had a talent for highbrow fare as well. He directed the Sherlock Holmes film *Murder by Decree*, which won five Genie Awards, including Best Achievement in Direction and Best Performance for leads Christopher Plummer and Geneviève Bujold. This was followed by a TV movie of the Bernard Slade play *Tribute*. Under Clark's direction, *Tribute* received 11 Genie nominations, and star Jack Lemmon received a Genie award for Best Performance plus a Best Actor Oscar® nomination.

Clark then turned to a longtime personal project based on his boyhood exploits in Florida. As co-writer, producer and director of 1982's *Porky's*, his trend-setting entertainment instincts were on target yet again, spawning a wildly successful new genre: the teen sex comedy. Clark wrote, produced and directed the film's first sequel, *Porky's II: The Next Day* (1983), but turned down involvement in the franchise's third installment, *Porky's Revenge*.

Clark's interest in *A Christmas Story* began in the late 1960s, when he heard a radio broadcast of Jean Shepherd recounting his childhood in Indiana. Clark was enthralled by the program and knew right away he wanted to make a movie out of the stories. Leonard Maltin described Shepherd and Clark's 1983 collaboration on *A Christmas Story* as "one of those rare movies you can say is perfect in every way." Clark has a cameo in the film as Swede, the neighbor who questions the Old Man about the Leg Lamp.

Bob Clark was active in the film industry until his death in 2007.

🌿 JEAN SHEPHERD 🌿

Raised in Hammond, Indiana, Jean "Shep" Shepherd worked in a steel mill and was a veteran of the Army Signal Corps before entering the arts in the late 1940s. These formative life experiences provided rich source material for a career in radio, publishing, music, television and film that spanned close to five decades.

A popular and prolific performer of the spoken word, Shepherd broadcast his trademark monologues on American life from such diverse venues as universities, jazz clubs and Carnegie Hall, often to sold-out crowds. The seventies saw him breaking ground in public television with an innovative program format in which he spun stories, visited unusual places and interviewed local personalities. His radio program at station WOR-AM in New York struck a deep chord in audiences, attracting many loyal listeners over twenty years.

Shepherd also published a series of books, including *Wanda Hickey's Night of Golden Memories*, *The Ferrari in the Bedroom* and *A Fistful of Fig Newtons*. His most well-known is *In God We Trust: All Others Pay Cash*, a comic novel based on a collection of semi-autobiographical short stories written for *Playboy* during the 1960s. These stories became the framework for the project *A Christmas Story*.

Co-written with Leigh Brown and Bob Clark and narrated by Shepherd himself, *A Christmas Story* tells the tale of nine-year-old Ralphie, who wants a Red Ryder BB gun for Christmas. The story's plain-spoken warmth and honest portrayal of parental foibles and childhood dreams have made it a beloved holiday classic. A sequel, *My Summer Story* (also known as *It Runs in the Family*), was made in 1994.

One of America's foremost humorists and most cherished storytellers, Shepherd's influence can be seen in the work of modern artists such as Spalding Gray, Garrison Keillor and Jerry Seinfeld. Jean Shepherd died in 1999 and was posthumously inducted into the National Radio Hall of Fame in 2005.

"CHRISTMAS WAS ON ITS WAY.

LOVELY, GLORIOUS, BEAUTIFUL CHRISTMAS,

UPON WHICH THE ENTIRE KID YEAR REVOLVED."

"I CAN'T PUT MY ARMS DOWN!"

"MY KID BROTHER LOOKED LIKE A TICK ABOUT TO POP!"

"WELL I DOUBLE-DOG-DARE YA!"

"NOW IT WAS SERIOUS.
A DOUBLE-DOG-DARE.
WHAT ELSE WAS THERE BUT A

'TRIPLE DARE YA'?

AND THEN, THE COUP DE GRÂCE OF ALL DARES,
THE SINISTER TRIPLE-DOG-DARE."

"I TRIPLE-DOG-DARE YA!"

"SCHWARTZ CREATED A SLIGHT
BREACH OF ETIQUETTE BY SKIPPING
THE TRIPLE DARE AND GOING
RIGHT FOR THE THROAT!"

Oatmeal-Cranberry Chocolate Chip Cookies

Dried cranberries add sweet, tart notes. These drop cookies would make a nice holiday gift.

INGREDIENTS

1 cup whole wheat flour (about 4 3/4 ounces)
1/4 cup all-purpose flour (about 1 ounce)
3/4 cup regular oats
1 teaspoon baking soda
1/2 teaspoon salt
1 1/2 cups packed brown sugar
1/4 cup butter, softened
1/4 cup reduced-fat sour cream
1 teaspoon vanilla extract
2 large egg whites
3/4 cup sweetened dried cranberries, coarsely chopped
1/2 cup semisweet chocolate chips

DIRECTIONS

Preheat oven to 350°.

Lightly spoon flour into dry measuring cups; level with a knife. Combine flour, oats, baking soda and salt in a medium bowl. Place sugar, butter and sour cream in a large bowl; beat with a mixer at high speed until smooth. Add vanilla and egg whites; beat well. Gradually add flour mixture, stirring until blended. Fold in cranberries and chocolate chips.

Drop dough by rounded teaspoonfuls 2 inches apart onto 2 baking sheets lined with parchment paper. Bake at 350° for 15 minutes or until edges of cookies are browned. Cool on pan 5 minutes. Remove cookies from pan; cool on wire racks.

Yield: 27 servings (serving size: 2 cookies)

Triple-Fruit Scones

Dried cranberries and apricots, as well as orange rind, give these scones a sweet, tart flavor. But you can mix and match any dried fruits to create your own fruit scone.

INGREDIENTS
3 cups all-purpose flour
1/3 cup sugar
1 tablespoon baking powder
1/2 teaspoon baking soda
1/4 teaspoon salt
6 tablespoons chilled stick margarine or butter
1/3 cup chopped dried apricots
1/3 cup sweetened dried cranberries (such as Craisins)
3/4 cup low-fat buttermilk
2 teaspoons grated orange rind
1 large egg
1 large egg white
Cooking spray
1 tablespoon sugar

DIRECTIONS
Preheat oven to 400°.

Lightly spoon flour into dry measuring cups; level with a knife. Combine flour, 1/3 cup sugar, baking powder, baking soda and salt; cut in margarine with a pastry blender or 2 knives until mixture resembles coarse meal. Stir in apricots and cranberries. Combine buttermilk, orange rind, egg and egg white; add to flour mixture, stirring just until moist.

Turn dough out onto a lightly floured surface; knead lightly 4 times with floured hands. Roll dough into a 12- x 6-inch rectangle. Cut dough into 8 (3-inch) squares using a dull knife or a dough scraper. Cut each square into 2 triangles; place on a baking sheet coated with cooking spray. Sprinkle with 1 tablespoon sugar; bake at 400° for 12 minutes or until golden. Serve warm.

Yield: 16 servings (serving size: 1 scone)

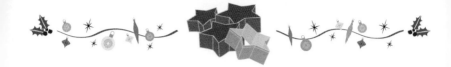

Caramel Fudge Cutouts
Candy thermometer required

INGREDIENTS
2 cups sugar
1/4 cup cocoa
3/4 cup milk
2 tablespoons light corn syrup
1/4 cup plus 2 tablespoons butter, divided
8 caramels, chopped
3/4 cup chopped skinned hazelnuts or pecans
2 teaspoons vanilla extract

DIRECTIONS
Line a 9" square pan with aluminum foil, allowing foil to extend over edges of pan.
Butter foil and set aside.

Butter insides of a heavy 3-quart saucepan. Combine sugar and cocoa in saucepan, stirring well. Stir in milk and corn syrup. Bring to a boil over medium-low heat, stirring gently and constantly with a wooden spoon, until sugar dissolves (6 to 8 minutes). Add 1/4 cup butter, stirring until butter melts.
Cover and boil 3 minutes over medium heat.

Uncover and cook, without stirring, until candy thermometer registers 238° (about 14 minutes). Remove from heat. Add remaining 2 tablespoons butter, chopped caramels, nuts and vanilla. Do not stir.
Let mixture cool to 130° (about 25 minutes).

Beat fudge by hand with a wooden spoon until it thickens and begins to lose its gloss (10 minutes).
Quickly spread fudge into prepared pan; let cool (about 3 hours). Lift uncut fudge out of pan with foil; discard foil, and place fudge on a cutting board. Cut desired shapes, using 2" cookie cutters,
or cut fudge into 1 1/2" squares.

Yield: 16 cutouts or 3 dozen squares

Pecan Sandies

It is important for your butter to be soft when you prepare the dough so it will hold together nicely when you shape it into balls.

INGREDIENTS
2 cups all-purpose flour (about 9 ounces)
1/4 cup finely chopped pecans
1/8 teaspoon salt
3/4 cup granulated sugar
9 tablespoons butter, softened
2 teaspoons vanilla extract
Cooking spray
1/4 cup powdered sugar

DIRECTIONS
Preheat oven to 350°.

Lightly spoon flour into dry measuring cups; level with a knife. Combine flour, pecans and salt, stirring well with a whisk.

Place granulated sugar and butter in a medium bowl; beat with a mixer at medium speed until fluffy (about 2 minutes). Beat in vanilla extract. Beating at low speed, gradually add flour mixture, and beat just until combined (mixture will be crumbly).

Shape dough into 34 (1-inch) balls (about 1 tablespoon each). Place dough balls 2 inches apart on baking sheets coated with cooking spray. Bake at 350° for 20 minutes or until lightly browned.

While cookies are still hot, sift powdered sugar evenly over tops. Remove from pan; cool completely on wire racks.

Yield: 34 cookies (serving size: 1 cookie)

"SCUT FARKUS STARING OUT AT US WITH HIS YELLOW EYES. HE HAD YELLOW EYES! SO, HELP ME, GOD! YELLOW EYES!"

"GROVER DILL!
SCUT FARKUS'
LITTLE TOADIE.
MEAN! ROTTEN!
HIS LIPS CURLED OVER
HIS GREEN TEETH."

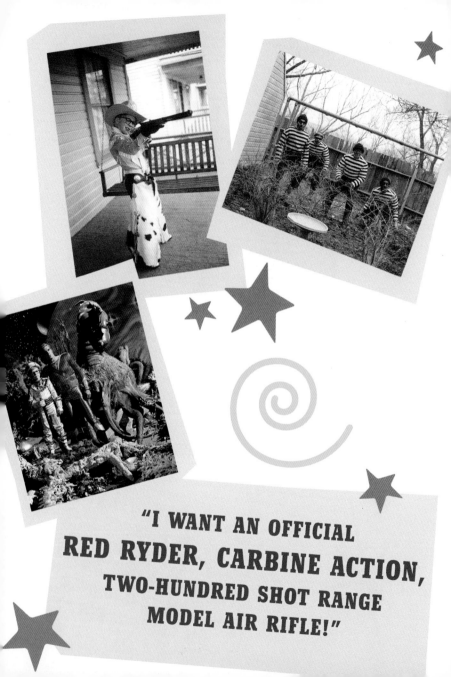

"I WANT AN OFFICIAL
RED RYDER, CARBINE ACTION,
TWO-HUNDRED SHOT RANGE
MODEL AIR RIFLE!"

Apple-Gingerbread Squares

INGREDIENTS

1/2 cup butter or margarine, softened
3/4 cup granulated sugar
1/3 cup firmly packed dark brown sugar
1 large egg
2 cups all-purpose flour
2 tablespoons crystallized ginger, minced
2 teaspoons ground ginger
1 1/2 teaspoons baking soda
1 teaspoon ground cinnamon
1 teaspoon ground cloves
1/2 teaspoon salt
1 cup molasses
1 cup boiling apple cider
Ginger-Molasses Whipped Cream

DIRECTIONS

Beat butter at medium speed with an electric mixer until creamy; gradually add granulated and brown sugars, beating well. Add egg, beating until mixture is blended.

Add flour and next 8 ingredients; beat at medium speed until smooth. Pour into a greased and floured 13- x 9-inch pan.

Bake at 325° for 35 to 45 minutes or until a wooden pick inserted in center comes out clean. Cool on a wire rack. Cut into 3-inch squares. Serve gingerbread with Ginger-Molasses Whipped Cream.

Yield: 12 servings

"YOU'LL SHOOT YOUR EYE OUT!"

Braised Red Cabbage

INGREDIENTS
1 medium-size red cabbage, thinly sliced
1/4 cup red wine vinegar
1 teaspoon salt
1/2 teaspoon pepper
4 bacon slices, diced
1 large onion, thinly sliced
2 apples, peeled and sliced
3/4 cup red wine
1/4 cup sugar
1/4 teaspoon minced garlic

DIRECTIONS
Toss together first 4 ingredients in a large bowl.
Cook bacon in a large Dutch oven over medium-high heat 10 minutes or until crisp.
Add onion and sauté 5 minutes or until tender.
Stir in cabbage mixture, apples, red wine, sugar and minced garlic.
Cover, reduce heat to medium, and simmer 30 to 35 minutes.

Yield: 6 servings

Old-fashioned Meatloaf

Prep: 20 min., Cook: 7 min., Bake: 1 hr., Stand 10 min.

INGREDIENTS
1 tablespoon butter
3 celery ribs, finely chopped
1/2 large onion, finely chopped
2 pounds lean ground beef
2 tablespoons Worcestershire sauce, divided
1/2 cup Italian-seasoned breadcrumbs
1/3 cup ketchup
2 teaspoons Creole seasoning
1 teaspoon Greek seasoning
1 teaspoon garlic powder
2 large eggs, lightly beaten
1 (8-ounce) can tomato sauce
3 tablespoons tomato paste
1 tablespoon ketchup
Garnish: chopped fresh flat-leaf parsley

DIRECTIONS
Melt butter in a medium nonstick skillet over medium heat; add celery and onion,
and sauté 7 minutes or just until tender.

Stir together celery mixture, ground beef, 1 tablespoon Worcestershire sauce,
breadcrumbs and next 5 ingredients in a large bowl. Shape into a 10- x 5-inch loaf;
place on a lightly greased broiler rack. Place rack in an aluminum foil-lined broiler pan.

Bake at 350° for 45 minutes. Stir together remaining 1 tablespoon Worcestershire sauce,
tomato sauce, tomato paste and 1 tablespoon ketchup until blended; pour evenly over
meatloaf, and bake 10 to 15 more minutes or until no longer pink in center.
Let stand 10 minutes before serving.

Note: For testing purposes only, we used Tony Chachere's Original Creole Seasoning
and Cavender's All Purpose Greek Seasoning.

Yield: 6 to 8 servings

"IT'S...IT'S...IT'S
INDESCRIBABLY BEAUTIFUL!
IT REMINDS ME OF
THE FOURTH OF JULY!"

Sugar Cookie Cutouts

Notes: Cookies can be made up to 3 days ahead; store airtight at room temperature (freeze to keep longer). Prep and cook time: About 45 minutes

INGREDIENTS

1 cup (1/2 lb.) butter, at room temperature
2/3 cup sugar
1 large egg
1 teaspoon vanilla
2 1/2 cups all-purpose flour
1/4 teaspoon salt
Royal icing

DIRECTIONS

In a large bowl, with an electric mixer on medium speed, beat butter and sugar until blended, then beat on high speed until creamy. Add egg and vanilla and beat until well blended.

Add flour and salt; beat on low speed until combined, then on medium speed until well blended. Divide dough into three equal portions.

Place each portion between sheets of floured plastic wrap. Press evenly into a disk about 1/4 inch thick. Stack disks on a baking sheet and chill until dough is firm, at least 15 minutes, or up to 2 days.

Working with one portion of dough at a time (keep remaining chilled), peel off plastic wrap and set disk on a floured board. With a floured rolling pin, roll dough about 1/8 inch thick. With floured cookie cutters (2 to 4 in. wide), cut out cookies, placing cutters as close together as possible. Transfer to baking parchment-lined or bare baking sheets (don't butter sheets), placing cookies about 1 inch apart. Gather up dough scraps and press together into a ball. If dough is still cold, roll and cut out remaining cookies. If dough is soft and sticky, press scraps into a ball and repeat step 3.

Bake cookies in a 350° oven (325° for convection) until golden around edges, 7 to 9 minutes. If baking more than one sheet at a time in one oven, switch positions halfway through baking. Slide parchment with cookies off sheets and onto racks or a counter to cool, then remove from parchment. Or cool on sheets about 1 minute, then, with a wide spatula, transfer cookies to racks to cool completely. If not using baking parchment, wipe off baking sheets after each batch. Cool sheets before filling with more cookies.

To decorate: Gather royal icing, cake-decorating sugar, jimmies, colored sprinkles, miniature chocolate chips and/or red-hot candies.

Fold down the top edges of a 1-quart heavy zip-lock plastic bag to form a cuff about 3 inches wide.

Hold the bag under cuff and scoop in 1 to 2 cups icing. Squeeze the icing down into one corner of the bag. Squeeze all the air out of bag, and seal.

When ready to use, cut about 1/16 inch off the filled corner of the plastic bag. Twist bag just above icing. Holding twisted end with one hand, gently press bag from the top to pipe icing onto cookie. Twist bag tighter as it empties. Sprinkle or gently press decorative sugar, candies or chocolate chips into soft icing.

When you're not using the icing bag, fold the opening closed and seal with a paper clip.

Let cookies stand until icing is firm, 30 to 45 minutes. Store iced cookies airtight up to 3 days.

Yield: About 5 dozen 2-inch cookies

Black-and-White Cookies

Big, irregular chunks of white chocolate look great in contrast to the dark, bittersweet chocolate in these cookies. Prep and cook time: 45 minutes, plus at least 1 hour to chill.

INGREDIENTS

12 ounces bittersweet or semisweet chocolate, chopped
3/4 cup (3/8 lb.) butter, cut into chunks
1 1/2 cups sugar
3 large eggs
2 teaspoons vanilla
2 1/4 cups all-purpose flour
1 1/2 teaspoons baking powder
1/2 teaspoon baking soda
1/2 teaspoon salt
8 to 10 ounces coarsely chopped white chocolate or 2 cups white chocolate chips

DIRECTIONS

Preheat oven to 325°.

In a heatproof bowl set over a pan of barely simmering water
(but not touching it), stir bittersweet chocolate and butter until smooth, 5 minutes.
Remove bowl from over water; whisk in sugar, eggs and vanilla.

In another bowl, mix flour, baking powder, baking soda and salt. Add to chocolate mixture
and stir until well blended. Stir in white chocolate. Cover and chill dough until firm, at least 1 hour.

Shape dough into 2-inch balls and place about 3 inches apart on buttered or cooking
parchment-lined 12- x 15-inch baking sheets.

Bake until set at the edges but still soft in the center, 12 to 15 minutes; if baking more than one
pan at a time, switch pan positions halfway through baking.

Let cool for 5 minutes on sheets; transfer to racks to cool completely.

Yield: About 28 cookies (serving size: 1 cookie)

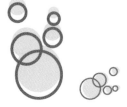

"OVER THE YEARS I GOT TO BE QUITE A **CONNOISSEUR** OF SOAP. THOUGH MY PERSONAL PREFERENCE WAS FOR LUX, I FOUND THAT PALMOLIVE HAD A NICE, PIQUANT AFTER-DINNER FLAVOR – HEAVY, BUT WITH A TOUCH OF MELLOW SMOOTHNESS. LIFE BUOY, ON THE OTHER HAND... **YECCHH!**"

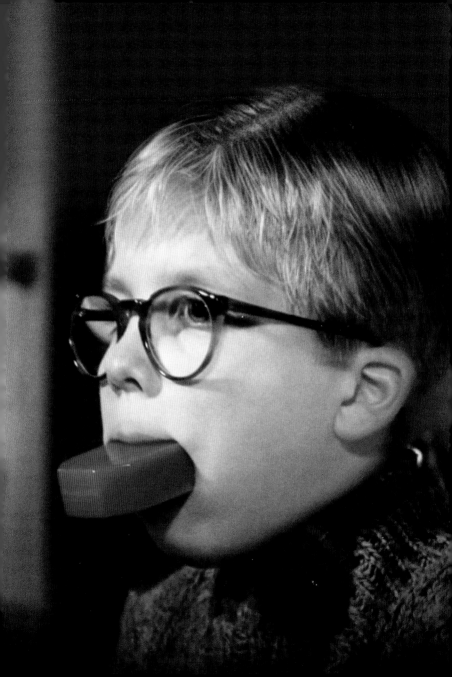

Santa's Shortbread Cookies

INGREDIENTS
1 cup butter, softened
3/4 cup powdered sugar
2 teaspoons vanilla extract
2 cups all-purpose flour
1/4 teaspoon baking powder
1/8 teaspoon salt

DIRECTIONS
Beat butter at medium speed with an electric mixer until creamy;
gradually add powdered sugar, beating well. Add vanilla, beating until blended.

Combine flour, baking powder and salt; add to butter mixture,
beating at low speed until blended.

Divide cookie dough in half; shape each portion into a 10-inch log. Wrap in wax paper, chill 8 hours;
or freeze up to 6 weeks, and thaw in refrigerator.

Cut each roll into 1/3-inch-thick slices; place on lightly greased baking sheets.

Bake at 350° for 10 to 12 minutes or until lightly browned. Transfer to wire racks to cool.

Chocolate-Dipped Shortbread Cookies: Microwave 1/2 cup semisweet chocolate morsels in a glass bowl at
HIGH 1 minute. Stir until smooth. Dip half of each cooled cookie into chocolate. Place on wax paper to set.

Chocolate-Mint Shortbread Cookies: Stir 1 (4.67-ounce) package chocolate mints, chopped,
into dough after adding flour mixture. Proceed as directed.

Toffee Shortbread Cookies: Stir 1 cup almond brickle chips into dough after adding flour mixture.
Proceed as directed. (For testing purposes only, we used Heath Bits o' Brickle chips, found near
chocolate chips in the grocery store.)

Pecan-Crusted Shortbread Cookies: Coat 10-inch logs with 3/4 cup finely chopped pecans.
Proceed as directed.

Red Cinnamon Candy Shortbread Cookies: Stir 1/2 cup red cinnamon candies into dough after adding
flour mixture. Proceed as directed.

Snowman Shortbread Cookies: Chill dough 2 hours after adding flour mixture. Shape dough into
16 (3/4-inch) balls, 16 (1/2-inch) balls and 16 (1/4-inch) balls. Use 1 ball of each size to make snowman
shapes, leaving no space between balls. Bake as directed. For eyes, use black gel frosting after cookies cool,
or press chocolate mini morsels onto warm cookies. Make scarves using
red decorator frosting after cookies cool.

Yield: 5 dozen

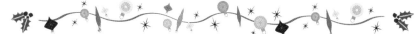

"HE LOOKS
LIKE A
DERANGED
EASTER BUNNY."

Eggnog Cheese Pie with Bourbon Cream

INGREDIENTS
Crust:
32 low-fat graham crackers (8 cookie sheets)
2 tablespoons granulated sugar
1 1/2 tablespoons butter, melted
1 large egg white
Cooking spray

Filling:
1/2 cup plain fat-free yogurt
1/2 cup (4-ounces) block-style 1/3-less-fat cream cheese, softened
1/2 cup (4-ounces) block-style fat-free cream cheese, softened
1 teaspoon vanilla extract
2 large eggs
1/3 cup granulated sugar
2 tablespoons all-purpose flour
1/8 teaspoon salt
2/3 cup eggnog
2 large egg whites
2 tablespoons granulated sugar

Bourbon cream:
3/4 cup frozen fat-free whipped topping, thawed
2 tablespoons eggnog
1 teaspoon bourbon
1/8 teaspoon grated nutmeg

DIRECTIONS
Preheat oven to 350°.

To prepare crust, place crackers in a food processor; process until crumbly. Add 2 tablespoons sugar, butter and 1 egg white; pulse 5 times or just until moist. Press crumb mixture evenly into a 9-inch pie plate coated with cooking spray. Bake at 350° for 8 minutes; cool on a wire rack for 15 minutes.

Reduce oven temperature to 325°.

To prepare filling, spoon yogurt onto several layers of heavy-duty paper towels; spread yogurt to 1/2-inch thickness. Cover with additional paper towels; let stand 5 minutes. Scrape into a bowl using a rubber spatula. Place cream cheeses and vanilla in a bowl; beat with mixer at medium speed until smooth. Add eggs, one at a time, beating well after each addition. Combine sugar, flour and salt, stirring with a whisk. Add sugar mixture to cheese mixture; beat until combined. Add yogurt to cheese mixture; add eggnog. Beat at low speed just until combined.

Beat 2 egg whites with a mixer at medium speed until soft peaks form. Add 2 tablespoons sugar, 1 tablespoon at a time, beating until stiff peaks form. Gently fold egg whites into the eggnog mixture. Pour filling into prepared crust. Bake at 325° for 40 minutes or until center is almost set. Cool completely on wire rack. Chill overnight.

To prepare bourbon cream, place the whipped topping in bowl. Gently fold in 2 tablespoons eggnog and bourbon; chill. Top each pie slice with bourbon cream; sprinkle with nutmeg before serving.

Yield: 10 servings (serving size: 1 pie slice and about 2 teaspoons bourbon cream)

Caramel-Pecan Pie

Prep: 20 min., Bake: 38 min., Cook: 7 min.

INGREDIENTS
1/2 (15-ounce) package refrigerated piecrusts
28 caramels
1/4 cup butter
1/4 cup water
3/4 cup sugar
2 large eggs
1/2 teaspoon vanilla extract
1/4 teaspoon salt
1 cup coarsely chopped pecans, toasted
Chocolate-Dipped Pecans (optional)

DIRECTIONS
Fit piecrust into a 9-inch pie plate according to package directions; fold edges under, and crimp. Prick bottom and sides of piecrust with a fork.

Bake piecrust at 400° for 6 to 8 minutes or until lightly browned; cool on wire rack.

Combine caramels, butter, and 1/4 cup water in large saucepan over medium heat. Cook, stirring constantly, 5 to 7 minutes or until caramels and butter are melted; remove from heat.

Stir together sugar and next 3 ingredients. Stir into caramel mixture until thoroughly combined. Stir in pecans. Pour into prepared crust.

Bake pie at 400° for 10 minutes. Reduce heat to 350°, and bake 20 more minutes, shielding edges of crust with aluminum foil to prevent excessive browning. Remove pie to a wire rack to cool. Top with Chocolate-Dipped Pecans, if desired.

Yield: 8 servings

"OH MY GOD, I SHOT MY EYE OUT!"

"THE HEAVENLY AROMA STILL
HUNG IN THE HOUSE.
BUT IT WAS GONE, ALL GONE!
NO TURKEY! NO TURKEY SANDWICHES!
NO TURKEY SALAD! NO TURKEY GRAVY!
TURKEY HASH! TURKEY A LA KING!
OR GALLONS OF TURKEY SOUP!
GONE, ALL GONE!"

The Perfect Holiday Turkey Dinner

Lemon-Sage Turkey with Wild Mushroom Gravy
Remember to reserve the drippings from the bottom of the pan.
You will use them to make the gravy.

INGREDIENTS

3 tablespoons grated lemon rind
1/4 cup fresh lemon juice
3 tablespoons dried thyme
2 tablespoons dried rubbed sage
1 tablespoon cracked black pepper
1 teaspoon salt
1 (12-pound) fresh or frozen turkey, thawed
2 (16-ounce) cans fat-free, less-sodium chicken broth
Cooking spray
Wild-Mushroom Gravy

DIRECTIONS

Combine first 6 ingredients; set aside.

Remove and discard giblets from turkey, reserving neck for gravy. Rinse turkey with cold water; pat dry. Trim excess fat. Starting at neck cavity, loosen skin from breast and drumsticks by inserting fingers, gently pushing between skin and meat. Lift wing tips up and over back; tuck under turkey. Rub spice mixture under loosened skin; rub into the body cavity.

Preheat oven to 350°.

Pour 1 can of broth in bottom of a shallow roasting pan. Place turkey, breast side up, on a rack coated with cooking spray. Place rack in roasting pan. Insert meat thermometer into meaty part of thigh, making sure not to touch bone. Bake at 350° for 1 1/2 hours. Carefully pour 1 can of broth into pan. Bake an additional 1 1/2 hours or until thermometer registers 180°. Remove turkey from oven; reserve pan drippings to make gravy. Cover turkey loosely with foil; let stand 15 to 20 minutes. Discard skin. Serve with Wild-Mushroom Gravy.

Yield: 12 servings (serving size: 6 ounces turkey and 1/4 cup gravy)

Sausage and Herb Stuffing

INGREDIENTS
2 tablespoons butter or stick margarine
2 (4-ounce) links sweet Italian turkey sausage, crumbled
2 cups chopped onion
2 cups chopped fennel bulb
1/2 cup chopped celery
3 garlic cloves, minced
1 1/2 cups fat-free, less-sodium chicken broth
1/3 cup chopped fresh parsley
1 1/2 teaspoons dried thyme
1 1/2 teaspoons dried oregano
1/2 teaspoon salt
12 cups (1-inch) cubed French bread (about 1 [1-pound] loaf)
1 cup thinly sliced green onions
1 large egg, lightly beaten
Cooking spray

DIRECTIONS
Preheat oven to 375°.

Melt the butter in a Dutch oven over medium-high heat. Add sausage; cook 4 minutes or until browned. Add chopped onion, fennel, celery and garlic; sauté 8 minutes.
Stir in broth and next 4 ingredients (broth through salt), scraping pan to loosen browned bits.
Remove from heat. Stir in bread, green onions and egg. Spoon into a 13- x 9-inch baking dish coated with cooking spray. Bake at 375° for 35 minutes.

Yield: 13 servings (serving size: 3/4 cup)

Roasted Mashed Potatoes with Leeks

INGREDIENTS
1 leek (about 1/2 pound)
8 1/2 cups cubed Yukon gold or red potatoes (about 3 pounds)
Cooking spray
1 1/2 tablespoons olive oil, divided
1 1/2 cups 1% low-fat milk
1 teaspoon salt
1/2 teaspoon black pepper
1 (8-ounce) carton low-fat sour cream

DIRECTIONS
Preheat oven to 425°.

Remove roots and outer leaves from leek, leaving 1-inch of green leaves. Discard remaining leaves; rinse with cold water. Remove 1-inch green leaves; cut lengthwise into 1-inch strips. Set aside. Cut white portion into thin slices to measure 1/2 cup.

Combine white portion of leek and potatoes in a 13- x 9-inch baking dish coated with cooking spray. Drizzle with 1 tablespoon oil; toss well. Place green portion of leek in an 8-inch baking dish. Drizzle with 1 1/2 teaspoons oil; toss well and set aside.

Bake potato mixture at 425° for 20 minutes, stirring once. (Do not remove from oven.) Add baking dish with green leek tops to oven. Bake at 425° for 15 minutes or until potato mixture and green leek tops are tender, stirring both after 8 minutes. Remove baking dishes from oven.

Place milk in a large microwave-safe bowl. Microwave at high 2 minutes or until warm. Add potato mixture; beat with mixer at medium speed until well-blended. Stir in salt, pepper and sour cream. Sprinkle with green leek tops.

Yield: 8 servings (serving size: 1 cup)

Gingerbread Cookies

INGREDIENTS
3/4 cup molasses
1/2 cup salad oil
1/3 cup firmly packed brown sugar
1 large egg
About 2 3/4 cups all-purpose flour
1/2 teaspoon salt
1 tablespoon baking powder
1 tablespoon ground cinnamon
1 tablespoon ground ginger
1/2 teaspoon ground cloves
Powdered Sugar Icing (recipe follows; optional)

DIRECTIONS
In a large bowl, with a mixer on medium speed, beat molasses, oil, brown sugar
and egg until well blended.

In a medium bowl, mix 2 3/4 cups flour, salt, baking powder, cinnamon, ginger and cloves. Stir into
molasses mixture, then beat until well blended. Divide dough in half, gather each half into a ball,
then flatten into a disk. Wrap each disk in plastic wrap and freeze until firm, about 1 hour.

Unwrap dough. On a lightly floured surface, with a floured rolling pin, roll one disk at a time to about
1/4 inch thick. With floured 3- to 4-inch cutters, cut out cookies. Place about 1 inch apart on buttered
12- x 15-inch baking sheets. Gather excess dough into a ball, reroll, and cut out remaining cookies.

Bake cookies at 350° in a regular or convection oven until edges begin to brown slightly,
8 to 10 minutes; if baking two sheets at once in one oven, switch their positions halfway through baking.
Let cookies cool on sheets for 5 minutes, then transfer to racks to cool completely.
Pipe Powdered Sugar Icing over cookies as desired.

Powdered Sugar Icing: In a bowl, stir 2 cups powdered sugar, 1 1/2 tablespoons water
and 1/2 teaspoon vanilla until smooth. Tint to desired color by stirring in food coloring,
a drop or two at a time. If icing is too thick to work with, stir in more water, a few drops at a time;
if too thin, stir in more powdered sugar. Makes 2/3 cup.

Yield: About 3 dozen 3- to 4-inch cookies

Chinese Turkey
20-Minute Peking Duck
*Here's a simplified – and delicious – Peking duck
with flour tortillas standing in for traditional thin pancakes.*

INGREDIENTS
2 teaspoons dark sesame oil
2 (8-ounce) packages boneless duck breast halves, thawed and skinned
1/3 cup hoisin sauce
1/2 teaspoon grated orange rind
2 tablespoons orange juice
2 teaspoons Sriracha (hot chili sauce, such as Huy Fong)
4 (6-inch) flour tortillas
1/2 cucumber, peeled, halved lengthwise, seeded and cut lengthwise into 8 strips
2 green onion tops, cut into thin strips
2 teaspoons sesame seeds

DIRECTIONS
Heat oil in a large nonstick skillet over medium-high heat.
Add duck to pan; cook 2 minutes on each side. Reduce heat to medium;
cover and cook an additional 3 minutes on each side or until done.
Cut duck diagonally across grain into thin slices.
Combine hoisin, orange rind, orange juice and Sriracha.
Heat tortillas according to package directions.
Spread about 2 tablespoons hoisin mixture down center of each tortilla.
Top each tortilla with 1/4 of duck, 2 cucumber strips,
1/4 of onions and 1/2 teaspoon sesame seeds; roll up.

Yield: 4 servings (serving size: 1 filled tortilla)

"IT'S A **BEAUTIFUL** DUCK.
IT REALLY IS.
BUT YOU SEE, IT'S SMILING AT ME."

PEACE.
HARMONY.
COMFORT AND JOY...
MAYBE NEXT YEAR.